# GREATEST INSPIRATIONAL QUOTES

365 days to more
Happiness, Success, and Motivation

Dr. Joe Tichio

ISBN-13: 978-1481900805
ISBN-10: 1481900803

Cover design by Erica Yates

# CONTENTS

# INTRODUCTION

It has always amazed me how powerful a few simple words can be. In the office I have often shared inspirational quotes with patients to lift their spirits and help them to refocus on the positive. The right words can provide needed encouragement, inspiration, and even permission to break free from a damaging situation.

Inspirational quotes are so effective because they are isolated pieces of information, not muddied or diluted by surrounding words or sentences. There is no context to the quote, other than the context of your life. This allows them to speak directly to your situation and act as powerful catalysts with life changing possibilities.

The pages that follow are a collection of quotes I've used and love. They've been influential in my life and I know they can have a positive impact on yours too. These quotes will help create clarity, discover passion, choose purpose, and inspire your every day.

This book is yours to read as you wish, but I highly recommend you take the 365 day journey and go one quote at a time. Cultivate your being with these inspiring words, allow them to take root deep in your spirit and express their hidden power.

Thank you,

Dr. Joe Tichio

# HOW TO GET THE MOST OUT OF THIS BOOK

The book has been designed to work in several ways:

1. It's a 365 day journey that you can start at any time. Read one quote a day, and allow that quote to be your inspiration for the entire day. Write it down, carry it with you, and read it often. Take a few minutes 2 - 3 times a day to jot down any ideas, thoughts, and feelings you have about the quote. You will be amazed at what discoveries you can have with this process.

2. You may read this book from beginning to end like any other book.

3. You may pick a number from 1 - 365 and see which quote you have selected and use that quote to inspire your day, as a focus for meditation and journaling, or to provide guidance when facing a difficult situation.

4. Enjoy the book as a useful resource to the greatest collection of inspirational quotes.

**Note:** The quotes in this book are collected from many sources and time periods. To respect the integrity of the authors' work, I have maintained the gender references as they were originally used. A quote may say he/him/his/man, but the quote is equally applicable to both genders and all people.

I made every reasonable effort to correctly attribute each quote to the original author, but in some cases it was impossible to identify who first spoke or wrote a particular quote. In some instances, I gave credit to a more recent rendition of the quote, while in others I chose the classic version. In some cases I could not clarify who actually originated a quote so those are attributed to unknown.

Some quotes have several similar derivations. To decide which one to use I took the liberty of choosing the version that best fit the essence of the book and would connect with the majority of readers.

# 365 DAYS OF INSPIRATIONAL QUOTES

### 1
No one can make you feel inferior
without your consent.
Never give it.
-Eleanor Roosevelt

### 2
You've got to follow your passion.
You've got to figure out what it is you love,
who you really are. And have the courage
to do that.  I believe that the only courage
anybody ever needs is the courage
to follow your own dreams.
-Oprah Winfrey

### 3
What the caterpillar calls the end of the world,
the master calls a butterfly.
-Richard Bach

4
Life is not about waiting for the storms to pass.
It's about learning how to dance in the rain.
-Vivian Greene

5
I have not failed.
I've just found 10,000 ways that won't work.
-Thomas A. Edison

6
It was a high counsel that I once heard
given to a young person,
always do what you are afraid to do.
-Ralph Waldo Emerson

7
We tend to forget that happiness doesn't come
as a result of getting something we don't have,
but rather of recognizing and appreciating
what we do have.
-Friedrich Koenig

# 8

Nobody can go back and start a new beginning,
but anyone can start today
and make a new ending.
-Maria Robinson

# 9

Take care of your body.
It's the only place you have to live.
-Jim Rohn

# 10

Death is not the greatest loss in life.
The greatest loss is what dies inside us
while we live.
-Norman Cousins

# 11

Love does not make the world go round.
Love is what makes the ride worthwhile.
-Franklin P. Jones

## 12
Seek opportunity, not security.
A boat in a harbor is safe,
but in time its bottom will rot out.
-H. Jackson Brown, Jr.

## 13
Patience is not the ability to wait,
but the ability to keep a good attitude
while waiting.
-Unknown

## 14
Courage is not the absence of fear,
but rather the judgment that something else
is more important than fear.
-Ambrose Redmoon

## 15
Remember that failure is an event, not a person.
-Zig Ziglar

## 16

Success is doing what you want, when you want,
where you want, with whom you want,
as much as you want.
-Anthony Robbins

## 17

Do not wait to strike till the iron is hot;
but make it hot by striking.
-William B. Sprague

## 18

If you don't like something change it;
if you can't change it,
change the way you think about it.
-Mary Engelbreit

## 19

The easiest thing in the world to be is you.
The most difficult thing to be
is what other people want you to be.
Don't let them put you in that position.
-Leo Buscaglia

20
Don't ask yourself
what the world needs;
ask yourself
what makes you come alive.
And then go and do that.
Because what the world needs
is people who have come alive.
-Harold Thurman

## 21
Most of the important things in the world
have been accomplished by people
who have kept on trying
when there seemed to be no hope at all.
-Dale Carnegie

## 22
Risk more than others think is safe.
Care more than others think is wise.
Dream more than others think is practical.
Expect more than others think is possible.
-Claude Bissell

## 23
I really don't think life is about the
I-could-have-beens.
Life is only about the I-tried-to-do.
I don't mind the failure, but
I can't imagine that I'd forgive myself if I didn't try.
-Nikki Giovanni

24
If you do not go after what you want,
you'll never have it.
If you do not ask, the answer will always be no.
If you do not step forward,
you will always be in the same place.
-Unknown


25
It is one of the most beautiful compensations of
this life that no man can sincerely try to help
another without helping himself.
-Ralph Waldo Emerson


26
You cannot change your destination overnight,
but you can change your direction overnight.
-Jim Rohn

27

When I was 5 years old,
my mom always told me
that happiness was the key to life.
When I went to school, they asked
me what I wanted to be
when I grew up.
I wrote down "happy".
They told me
I didn't understand the assignment
and I told them
they didn't understand life.
-John Lennon

## 28

Somebody should tell us, right at the start of our lives, that we are dying.
Then we might live life to the limit, every minute of every day. Do it! I say.
Whatever you want to do, do it now!
There are only so many tomorrows.
-Pope Paul VI

## 29

Dream lofty dreams, and as you dream, so you shall become. Your vision is the promise of what you shall one day be; your ideal is the prophecy of what you shall at last unveil.
-James Allen

## 30

The optimist sees the rose and not its thorns; the pessimist stares at the thorns, oblivious of the rose.
-Kahlil Gibran

# 31

Positive thinking will let you do everything better
than negative thinking will.

-Zig Ziglar

# 32

What lies behind us and what lies before us
are tiny matters compared to what lies within us.

-Ralph Waldo Emerson

# 33

Touch a thistle timidly, and it pricks you;
grasp it boldly, and its spines crumble.

-Admiral William Halsey, Jr.

# 34

We must overcome the notion that we must be
regular, it robs you of the chance to be
extraordinary and leads you to the mediocre.

-Uta Hagen

## 35

For a long time it seemed to me that real life was about to begin - real life. But there was always some obstacle in the way. Something had to be got through first, some unfinished business, time still to be served, or a debt to be paid. Then life would begin. At last it dawned on me that these obstacles were my life.
-Father Alfred D'Souza

## 36

Inaction breeds doubt and fear.
Action breeds confidence and courage.
If you want to conquer fear,
do not sit home and think about it.
Go out and get busy.
-Dale Carnegie

## 37

It is not because things are difficult
that we do not dare,
it is because we do not dare
that they are difficult.
-Seneca

38
Figure out who you are separate from your family,
and the man or woman you're in a relationship
with. Find who you are in this world
and what you need to feel good alone.
I think that's the most important thing in life.
Find a sense of self because with that,
you can do anything else.
-Angelina Jolie


39
The minute you choose to do what you really
want to do, it's a different kind of life.
-Buckminster Fuller


40
It's not whether you get knocked down.
It's whether you get up again.
-Vince Lombardi

# 41
I don't want to get to the end of my life
and find that I lived just the length of it.
I want to have lived the width of it as well.
-Diane Ackerman

# 42
I gave myself permission to fail.
But I wouldn't give myself permission not to try.
-Steve Pavlina

# 43
You gain strength, courage, and confidence
by every experience in which you really stop to
look fear in the face. You must do the thing which
you think you cannot do.
-Eleanor Roosevelt

# 44
Let your friends, colleagues and family know
about the good that you see;
it will help them see it too.
-Unknown

### 45
You are never too old
to set another goal or to dream a new dream.
-C.S. Lewis

### 46
A happy person is not a person in a certain set of
circumstances, but rather a person with a certain
set of attitudes.
-Hugh Downs

### 47
Each moment of the year has its own beauty,
a picture which was never before
and shall never be seen again.
-Ralph Waldo Emerson

### 48
If you obey all the rules, you miss all the fun.
-Katharine Hepburn

49
Just don't give up trying to do
what you really want to do.
Where there is love and inspiration,
I don't think you can go wrong.
-Ella Fitzgerald

50
Life shrinks or expands
in proportion to one's courage.
-Anais Nin

51
Many of life's failures
are people who did not realize
how close they were to success
when they gave up.
-Thomas A Edison

52
Whatever you can do,
or dream you can do, begin it.
Boldness has genius, power, and magic in it.
-Johann Wolfgang von Goethe

## 53

You see, in life, lots of people know what to do,
but few people actually do what they know.
Knowing is not enough! You must take action.
-Anthony Robbins

## 54

Too many talented people
string and unstring their instruments
without ever playing their music.
-Unknown

## 55

Life is a grindstone,
and whether it grinds you down
or polishes you up
is for you and you alone to decide.
-Cavett Robert

56
Your only obligation in any lifetime
is to be true to yourself.
-Richard Bach

## 57

If one advances confidently in the direction of his dreams, and endeavors to live the life he has imagined, he will meet with a success unexpected in common hours.

-Henry David Thoreau

## 58

Challenges are what make life interesting; overcoming them is what makes life meaningful.

-Joshua J. Marine

## 59

The journey is what brings us happiness not the destination.

-Dan Millman

## 60
Security is mostly a superstition.
It does not exist in nature, nor do the children of
men as a whole experience it.
Avoiding danger is no safer in the long run
than outright exposure.
Life is either a daring adventure, or nothing.
-Helen Keller


## 61
The best way to succeed
is to double your failure rate.
-Thomas J. Watson


## 62
You never know when a moment
and a few sincere words
can have an impact on a life.
-Zig Ziglar


## 63
First say to yourself what you would be;
and then do what you have to do.
-Epictetus

# 64
To be upset over what you don't have
is to waste what you do have.
-Ken S. Keyes, Jr.

# 65
You don't get to choose how you're going to die.
Or when.
But you can decide how you're going to live now.
-Joan Baez

# 66
It is not the strongest of the species that survive,
nor the most intelligent, but the one most
responsive to change.
-Leon C. Megginson

# 67
Optimism is the one quality more associated with
success and happiness than any other.
-Brian Tracy

68
What you do is what matters,
not what you think or say or plan.
-Jason Fried/ David Heinemeier Hansson

69
By banishing doubt and trusting your intuitive
feelings, you clear a space for the power of
intention to flow through.
-Wayne Dyer

70
Snowflakes are one of nature's most fragile things,
but just look at what they can do
when they stick together.
-Vesta Kelly

# 71

Your time is limited, so don't waste
it living someone else's life.
Don't be trapped by dogma,
which is living with the results of
other people's thinking.
Don't let the noise of other's
opinions drown out
your own inner voice.
And most important,
have the courage to follow your
heart and intuition.
They somehow already know
what you truly want to become.
Everything else is secondary.
-Steve Jobs

72
Success is not the key to happiness.
Happiness is the key to success.
If you love what you are doing,
you will be successful.
-Albert Schweitzer

73
At bottom every man knows well enough that he
is a unique being, only once on this earth; and by
no extraordinary chance will such a marvelously
picturesque piece of diversity in unity as he is,
ever be put together a second time.
-Friedrich Nietzsche

74
People may doubt what you say,
but they will believe what you do.
-Lewis Cass

75
To live a creative life,
we must lose our fear of being wrong.
-Joseph Chilton Pearce

76
Trust yourself. You know more
than you think you do.
-Benjamin Spock


77
There are only 3 colors, 10 digits, and 7 notes;
it's what we do with them that's important.
-Jim Rohn


78
Courage doesn't mean you don't get afraid.
Courage means you don't let fear stop you.
-Bethany Hamilton


79
We don't stop playing because we grow old;
we grow old because we stop playing.
-George Bernard Shaw

# 80
I've missed more than 9000 shots in my career.
I've lost almost 300 games.
Twenty-six times I've been trusted to take the
game winning shot and missed.
I've failed over and over and over again in my life.
And that is why I succeed.
-Michael Jordan

# 81
When it is obvious that the goals cannot be
reached, don't adjust the goals,
adjust the action steps.
-Confucius

# 82
Time is all you have.
And you may find one day
that you have less than you think.
-Randy Pausch

83
Don't worry, be happy.
-Bobby McFerrin

84
Too many people are thinking of security instead
of opportunity. They seem more afraid of life
than death.
-James F. Byrnes

85
The entire water of the sea can't sink a ship unless
it gets inside the ship. Similarly, negativity of the
world can't put you down unless you allow it to
get inside you.
-Unknown

86
When we speak we are afraid our words
will not be heard or welcomed.
But when we are silent, we are still afraid.
So it is better to speak.
-Audre Lorde

## 87

You can only become truly accomplished at
something you love.  Don't make money your
goal.  Instead, pursue the things you love doing,
and then do them so well that people
can't take their eyes off you.
-Maya Angelou


## 88

Only put off until tomorrow
what you are willing to die having left undone.
-Pablo Picasso


## 89

Never mistake knowledge for wisdom.
One helps you make a living;
the other helps you make a life.
-Sandra Carey


## 90

The world is full of dreamers, there aren't enough
who will move ahead and begin to take concrete
steps to actualize their vision.
-W. Clement Stone

# 91

Discovery consists of seeing what everybody has seen and thinking what nobody has thought.

-Albert Szent-Györgyi

# 92

The thing that is really hard, and really amazing, is giving up on being perfect and beginning the work of becoming yourself.

-Anna Quindlen

# 93

Fear is not real.
It is a product of thoughts you create.
Now do not misunderstand me,
danger is very real,
but fear is a choice.

-Cypher Raige

# 94

Live your life as an exclamation,
not an explanation.

-H. Jackson Brown, Jr.

## 95
Work like you don't need the money,
love like your heart has never been broken,
and dance like no one is watching.
-Aurora Greenway


## 96
If you have made mistakes, even serious ones,
there is always another chance for you.
What we call failure is not the falling down,
but the staying down.
-Mary Pickford


## 97
The world you desired can be won,
it exists, it is real, it is possible, it's yours.
-Ayn Rand


## 98
Some people walk in the rain.
Others just get wet.
-Roger Miller

## 99
The pessimist sees difficulty in every opportunity.
The optimist sees the opportunity
in every difficulty.
-Winston Churchill

## 100
You must be the change
you wish to see in the world.
-Mahatma Gandhi

## 101
Every really new idea looks crazy at first.
-Alfred North Whitehead

## 102
To accomplish great things,
we must not only act, but also dream;
not only plan, but also believe.
-Anatole France

103
The men who try to do something and fail
are infinitely better than those who
try to do nothing and succeed.
-Lloyd Jones


104
Don't let what you cannot do
interfere with what you can do.
-John Wooden


105
If you light a lamp for someone else
it will also brighten your path.
-Buddha

106
Find out who you are and do it on purpose.
-Dolly Parton

107
The future belongs to those
who believe in the beauty of their dreams.
-Eleanor Roosevelt

108
Experience is not what happens to you;
it is what you do with what happens to you.
-Aldous Huxley

109
Those who dance
are considered insane
by those who can't hear the music.
-George Carlin

# 110
Our greatest fear should not be of failure,
but of succeeding at things in life
that don't really matter
-Francis Chan

# 111
If a man does not know which port he is steering
for, no wind is favorable to him.
-Seneca

# 112
When you change the way you look at things,
the things you look at change.
-Wayne Dyer

# 113
Nothing has to happen for me to feel good!
I feel good because I'm alive!
Life is a gift, and I revel in it.
-Anthony Robbins

## 114
Don't judge each day by the harvest you reap,
but by the seeds you plant.
-Robert Louis Stevenson

## 115
If you look at what you have in life,
you'll always have more.
If you look at what you don't have in life,
you'll never have enough.
-Oprah Winfrey

## 116
It is better to be a lion for a day,
than a sheep all your life.
-Elizabeth Kenny

# 117
Don't be afraid to give your best to what seemingly are small jobs. Every time you conquer one it makes you that much stronger. If you do the little jobs well, the big ones will tend to take care of themselves.
-Dale Carnegie

# 118
It's not what you look at that matters, it's what you see.
-Henry David Thoreau

# 119
The death rate for people who play it safe and for people who live boldly is the same: 100%
-Patti Digh

# 120
We are what we repeatedly do. Excellence, then, is not an act, but a habit.
-Aristotle

121
Man's most valuable faculty is his imagination.
-Unknown

122
Never let the odds keep you from doing
what you know in your heart
you were meant to do.
-H. Jackson Brown, Jr.

123
Life is not measured by the number of breaths we
take, but by the moments that
take our breath away.
-Unknown

124
There is no failure.
Only feedback.
-Robert Allen

# 125

Experience life in all possible ways
good-bad, bitter-sweet,
dark-light, summer-winter.
Experience all the dualities.
Don't be afraid of experience,
because the more experience you have,
the more mature you become.
-Osho

# 126

Happiness is an attitude.
We either make ourselves miserable,
or happy and strong.
The amount of work is the same.
-Francesca Reigler

# 127

If you want something you've never had,
then you've got to do something
you've never done.
-Unknown

128

If you view all the things that happen to you,
both good and bad, as opportunities, then you
operate out of a higher level of consciousness.
-Les Brown

129

Where there is no struggle, there is no strength.
-Oprah Winfrey

130

Do just once what others say you can't do,
and you will never pay attention to their
limitations again.
-James Cook

131

Watch your thoughts; they become words.
Watch your words; they become actions.
Watch your actions; they become habits.
Watch your habits; they become character.
Watch your character; it becomes your destiny.
-Unknown

## 132

Darkness cannot drive out darkness;
only light can do that.
Hate cannot drive out hate;
only love can do that.
-Martin Luther King, Jr.

## 133

I am an artist at living,
my work of art is my life.
-D.T. Suzuki

## 134

Knowing others is intelligence;
knowing yourself is true wisdom.
Mastering others is strength;
mastering yourself is true power.
-Lao Tzu

135
Life is short, live it.
Love is rare, grab it.
Anger is bad, dump it.
Fear is awful, face it.
Memory is sweet, cherish it.
-Unknown

136
Fortune favors the brave.
-Terence


137
In one minute you can change your attitude
and in that minute you can change
your entire day.
-Spencer Johnson


138
Success is never permanent,
and failure is never final.
-Mike Ditka


139
Live out of your imagination
instead of out of your memory.
-Les Brown

140
The minute you settle for less than you deserve,
you get even less than you settled for.
-Maureen Dowd


141
Never be afraid to try something new;
remember amateurs built the ark,
professionals built the Titanic.
-Unknown


142
There are so many wizards
of the computer, stock market,
test tube, and spectator sport,
but so few of the art of life.
-Mantak Chia


143
Life isn't about finding yourself.
Life is about creating yourself.
-George Bernard Shaw

144
What is now proved was once imagined.
-William Blake


145
When I was born I cried
while those around me smiled.
May I live my life so that when I die,
I may smile, while those around me cry.
-Unknown


146
The trick is in what one emphasizes.
We either make ourselves miserable,
or we make ourselves happy.
The amount of work is the same.
-Carlos Castaneda


147
Everything you want
is just outside your comfort zone.
-Robert Allen

148
As you climb the ladder of success,
check occasionally to make sure it is leaning
against the right wall.
-Unknown

149
Life is what happens to you
while you're busy making other plans.
-John Lennon

150
Don't be afraid your life will end;
be afraid that it will never begin.
-Grace Hansen

151
The greatest discovery of my generation
is that a human being can alter his life
by altering his attitudes.
-William James

## 152
The bitterest tears shed over graves
are for words left unsaid and deeds left undone.
-Harriet Beecher Stowe

## 153
You cannot always control what goes on outside.
But you can always control what goes on inside.
-Wayne Dyer

## 154
You were born an original.
Don't die a copy.
-John Mason

## 155
It's only when we truly know and understand that
we have a limited time on earth, and that we have
no way of knowing when our time is up, we will
then begin to live each day to the fullest,
as if it was the only one we had.
-Elisabeth Kubler-Ross

### 156
Dance for yourself, if someone understands, good.
If not then no matter,
go right on doing what you love.
-Lois Hurst

### 157
Our greatest glory is not in never failing,
but in rising every time we fail.
-Confucius

### 158
In order to live free and happily,
you must sacrifice boredom.
It is not always an easy sacrifice.
-Richard Bach

### 159
Happiness is not a station you arrive at,
but a manner of traveling.
-Margaret B. Runbeck

## 160
Smooth seas do not make skillful sailors.
-Proverb

## 161
Great spirits have always encountered
violent opposition from mediocre minds.
-Albert Einstein

## 162
Ancient Egyptians believed that upon death
they would be asked two questions and their
answers would determine whether they could
continue their journey in the afterlife.
The first question was, "Did you bring joy?"
The second was, "Did you find joy?"
-Leo Buscaglia

## 163
Always be a first-rate version of yourself,
instead of a second-rate version
of somebody else.
-Judy Garland

### 164
Let others lead small lives, but not you.
Let others argue over small things, but not you.
Let others cry over small hurts, but not you.
Let others leave their future in someone else's
hands, but not you.
-Jim Rohn

### 165
People are not disturbed by things,
but by the view they take of them.
-Epictetus

### 166
When faced with a challenge,
look for a way, not a way out.
-David Weatherford

### 167
Aerodynamically the bumblebee shouldn't be able
to fly, but the bumblebee doesn't know that
so it goes on flying anyway.
-Mary Kay Ash

168
Some people are so afraid to die
that they never begin to live.
-Henry Van Dyke


169
I'd rather regret the things that I have done
than the things that I have not done.
-Lucille Ball


170
Do you give as much energy to your dreams
as you do to your fears?
-Unknown


171
By being yourself, you put something wonderful in
the world that was not there before.
-Edwin Elliot

172
You may be hurt if you love too much,
but you will live in misery if you love too little.
-Napoleon Hill

173
Just do it!
-Nike

174
If it's never our fault,
we can't take responsibility for it.
If we can't take responsibility for it,
we'll always be its victim.
-Richard Bach

175
Be who you are and say what you feel,
because those who mind don't matter,
and those who matter won't mind.
-Dr. Seuss

## 176

The only way to do great work is to love what you do. If you haven't found it yet, keep looking. Don't settle. As with all matters of the heart, you'll know when you find it.
-Steve jobs

## 177

Every choice you make is creating your future. Choose wisely.
-Joe Tichio

## 178

A hero is no braver than an ordinary man, but he is braver five minutes longer.
-Ralph Waldo Emerson

179
Love the life you live.
Live the life you love.
-Bob Marley

180
Success is not final, failure is not fatal:
it is the courage to continue that counts.
-Winston Churchill

181
Learn from yesterday,
live for today,
hope for tomorrow.
-Albert Einstein

182
A goal is not always meant to be reached,
it often serves simply as something to aim at.
-Bruce Lee

183
Happiness is not something you postpone for the
future; it is something you design for the present.
-Jim Rohn

184
The groundwork of all happiness is health.
-Leigh Hunt

185
You are what you love,
not what loves you.
-Donald Kaufman

186
The key is not to prioritize what's on your
schedule, but to schedule your priorities.
-Stephen Covey

187
Anyone can sympathize with the sufferings of a
friend, but it requires a very fine nature
to sympathize with a friend's success.
-Oscar Wilde

## 188

Man's mind once stretched to a new idea,
never goes back to its original dimensions.
-Oliver Wendell Holmes

## 189

Taking time to do nothing
often brings everything into perspective.
-Doe Zantamata

## 190

Every strike brings me closer
to the next home run.
-Babe Ruth

## 191

Positive or negative, the beliefs we identify with
will result in any number of effects
that will dominate and shape our lives.
-Peter Ralston

192
Any fact facing us is not as important as our
attitude toward it, for that determines
our success or failure.
-Norman Vincent Peale


193
Somewhere along the line
we stopped believing we could do anything.
And if we don't have our dreams,
we have nothing.
-Charles Farmer


194
There are no great people in this world,
only great challenges which ordinary people
rise to meet.
-Admiral William Halsey, Jr.


195
Being realistic is the most commonly traveled road
to mediocrity.
-Will Smith

## 196

We seem to gain wisdom more readily
through our failures than through our successes.
We always think of failure as the antithesis of
success, but it isn't.  Success often lies just the
other side of failure.
-Leo Buscaglia


## 197

Set goals that make you feel powerful, motivated,
and driven when you focus on them.
-Steve Pavlina


## 198

Two sure ways to fail-
Think and never do or do and never think.
-Zig Ziglar


## 199

The most radical act anyone can commit
is to be happy.
-Patch Adams

## 200
The greatest wealth is health.
-Virgil

## 201
Love comes when manipulation stops;
when you think more about the other person
than about his or her reactions to you.
When you dare to reveal yourself fully.
When you dare to be vulnerable.
-Dr. Joyce Brothers

## 202
Give me six hours to chop down a tree
and I will spend the first four sharpening the axe.
-Abraham Lincoln

## 203
No matter how many mistakes you make
or how slow you progress,
you are still way ahead
of everyone who isn't trying.
-Anthony Robbins

## 204
Don't be pushed by your problems;
be led by your dreams.
-Unknown

## 205
The pain you feel today
is the strength you feel tomorrow.
-Unknown

## 206
It is the mark of an educated mind
to be able to entertain a thought
without accepting it.
-Aristotle

## 207
A journey of a thousand miles
must begin with a single step.
-Lao Tzu

## 208
Life is not a process of discovery,
but a process of creation.
-Neale Donald Walsch

## 209
It is better to be hated for what you
are than to be loved for something you are not.
-Andre Gide

## 210
To dare is to lose one's footing momentarily.
To not dare is to lose oneself.
-Soren Kierkegaard

## 211
Motivation is what gets you started.
Habit is what keeps you going.
-Jim Rohn

# 212
If you love life, don't waste time,
for time is what life is made up of.
-Bruce Lee

# 213
Giving into fear doesn't keep you safe,
it keeps you from trying, learning, and succeeding.
-Joe Tichio

# 214
Neither failure nor success has the power
to change your inner state of being.
-Eckhart Tolle

# 215
Take time to enjoy the little things,
for one day you may look back
and realize they were the big things.
-Robert Brault

# 216
The sexiest curve on your body
is your smile.
Flaunt it!
-Unknown

217
I want to love you without clutching,
appreciate you without judging,
join you without invading,
invite you without demanding,
leave you without guilt,
criticize you without blaming,
and help you without insulting.
If I can have the same from you,
then we can truly meet and enrich each other.
-Virginia Satir


218
Don't cry because it's over.
Smile because it happened.
-Dr Seuss


219
Risks must be taken,
because the greatest hazard in life
is to risk nothing.
-Leo Buscaglia

220
Each time we face our fear,
we gain strength, courage,
and confidence in the doing.
-Unknown

221
Life is different when we discover
what is deeply important to us.
-Stephen Covey

222
Answer these questions often:
What are you doing?
Why are you doing it?
Where is this going?
-Jed McKenna

223
One day you will wake up
and there won't be any more time
to do the things you've always wanted.
Do it now.
-Paulo Coelho

224
The easiest thing is to react.
The second easiest is to respond.
But the hardest thing is to initiate.
-Seth Godin

225
Seek not to follow in the footsteps of men of old;
seek what they sought.
-Matsuo Basho

226
Life is a big canvas,
throw all the paint on it you can.
-Danny Kaye

227
It's never too late
to be what you might have been.
-George Elliot


228
You always do what you want to do.
This is true with every act.
You may say that you had to do something,
or that you were forced to,
but actually, whatever you do, you do by choice.
Only you have the power to choose for yourself.
-W. Clement Stone


229
Example is not the main thing in influencing
others, it is the only thing.
-Albert Schweitzer


230
Life is 10% what happens to me
and 90% how I react to it.
-Charles Swindoll

## 231

Regret for the things we did can be tempered by time; it is regret for the things we did not do that is inconsolable.
-Sydney J. Harris

## 232

Normal day, let me be aware of the treasure you are. Let me not pass you by in quest of some rare and perfect tomorrow.
-Mary Jean Irion

## 233

The biggest mistake of man
is that he thinks he doesn't deserve
the good and the bad things from his life.
-Paulo Coelho

## 234

I fear not the man who has practiced 10,000 kicks once, but I fear the man who has practiced one kick 10,000 times.
-Bruce Lee

## 235
Courage is resistance to fear, mastery of fear,
not absence of fear.
-Mark Twain

## 236
Hoping means seeing that the outcome you want
is possible, and then working for it.
-Bernie Siegel

## 237
The block of granite which was an obstacle in the
pathway of the weak becomes a stepping stone in
the pathway of the strong.
-Thomas Carlyle

## 238
Time is more valuable than money.
You can get more money,
but you cannot get more time.
-Jim Rohn

# 239
You never lose by loving.
You always lose by holding back.
-Barbara De Angelis

240
If I had to live my life again,
I'd make the same mistakes, only sooner.
-Tallulah Bankhead


241
Trust your own instinct.
Your mistakes might as well be your own,
instead of someone else's.
-Billy Wilder


242
A hundred years from now it will not matter
what my bank account was, the sort of house I
lived in, or the kind of car I drove...
but the world may be different because I was
important in the life of a child.
- Forest E. Witcraft

## 243

Happiness is not determined by what's happening around you, but rather what's happening inside you. Most people depend on others to gain happiness, but the truth is, it always comes from within.

-Unknown

## 244

I slept and I dreamed that life is all joy.
I woke and I saw that life is all service.
I served and I saw that service is joy.

- Kahlil Gibran

## 245

When everything seems to be going against you, remember that the airplane takes off against the wind, not with it.

-Henry Ford

## 246

Don't sweat the small stuff...and it's all small stuff.

-Richard Carlson

247
Only the ideas we actually live are of any value.
-Hermann Hesse

248
Eighty percent of success is showing up.
-Woody Allen

249
You're tougher than you think you are,
and you can do more than you think you can.
-Christopher McDougall

250
Until a person can say deeply and honestly,
"I am what I am today because of the choices I
made yesterday," that person cannot say,
"I choose otherwise".
-Stephen Covey

## 251
When you don't know what you believe,
everything becomes an argument.
Everything is debatable.
But when you stand for something,
decisions are obvious.
-Jason Fried/ David Heinemeier Hansson

## 252
The key question to keep asking is,
are you spending your time on the right things?
Because time is all you have.
-Randy Pausch

## 253
Work as though you would live forever,
and live as though you would die today.
-Og Mandino

## 254
Courage is never to let your actions
be influenced by your fears.
-Arthur Koestler

255
To be nobody but yourself in a world which is
doing its best, night and day, to make you
everybody else means to fight the hardest battle
which any human being can fight;
and never stop fighting.
-E.E. Cummings


256
Remember that everyone you meet is afraid of
something, loves something,
and has lost something.
-Proverb


257
Employ your time in improving yourself
by other men's writings, so that you shall gain
easily what others have labored hard for.
-Socrates


258
The days are long, but the years are short.
-Unknown

259

We will discover the nature of our particular
genius when we stop trying to conform to our
own or other people's models, learn to be
ourselves, and allow our natural channel to open.
-Shakti Gawain


260

Remember, happiness doesn't depend
upon who you are or what you have,
it depends solely upon what you think.
-Dale Carnegie


261

Do not follow where the path may lead.
Go instead where there is no path
and leave a trail.
-Ralph Waldo Emerson


262

There is no such thing as failure.
There are only results.
-Anthony Robbins

## 263
What would you do if you weren't afraid?
-Spencer Johnson


## 264
The game of life is a game of boomerangs.
Our thoughts, deeds and words
return to us sooner or later
with astounding accuracy.
-Florence Scovel Shinn


## 265
Don't let life discourage you;
everyone who got where he is
had to begin where he was.
-Richard L. Evan


## 266
What you do every day matters more
than what you do once in a while.
-Gretchen Rubin

267

Success is going from failure to failure
without losing your enthusiasm.
-Winston Churchill

268

Nothing in the world is ever completely wrong.
Even a stopped clock is right twice a day.
-Paulo Coelho

269

You've achieved success in your field
when you don't know whether
what you're doing is work or play.
-Warren Beatty

270

Twenty years from now you will be more
disappointed by the things that you didn't do than
by the ones you did do.  So throw off the
bowlines.  Sail away from the safe harbor.
Catch the trade winds in your sails.
Explore. Dream. Discover.
-Mark Twain

271
Give whatever you are doing and whoever you are
with the gift of your attention.
-Jim Rohn

272
The greatest good you can do for another
is not just to share your riches
but to reveal to him his own.
-Benjamin Disraeli

273
At any given moment
you have the power to say
this is not how the story is going to end.
-Unknown

274
When you feel like giving up,
remember why you held on for so long
in the first place.
-Unknown

# 275

Be weird. Be random.
Be who you are.
Because you never know
who would love
the person you hid.
-Unknown

276
This too shall pass.
-Proverb

277
Getting what you want
and avoiding what you don't want
is not happiness. It's self survival.
-Peter Ralston

278
A ship is safe in harbor,
but that is not what ships are built for.
-Unknown

279
Experience is what you get
when you didn't get what you wanted.
And experience is often the most valuable thing
you have to offer.
-Randy Pausch

### 280
Life is not always a matter of holding good cards,
but sometimes, in playing a poor hand well.
-Robert Louis Stevenson


### 281
I do not think there is any other quality
so essential to success of any kind
as the quality of perseverance.
It overcomes almost everything, even nature.
-John D. Rockefeller


### 282
All things are possible until they are proved
impossible and even the impossible may only be
so, as of now.
-Pearl S. Buck

283
Stop acting as if life is a rehearsal.
Live this day as if it were your last.
The past is over and gone.
The future is not guaranteed.
-Wayne Dyer


284
The worst thing that can happen to you
is not striving for what you want.
-Jake Steinfeld


285
Give today all you have,
tomorrow will take care of itself.
-Unknown


286
If you can find a path with no obstacles,
it probably doesn't lead anywhere.
-Frank Clark

### 287
If you wait to do everything until you're sure it's right, you'll probably never do much of anything.
-Unknown

### 288
All endings are also beginnings.
We just don't know it at the time.
-Mitch Albom

### 289
You may be disappointed if you fail,
but you are doomed if you don't try.
-Beverly Sills

### 290
The world has the habit of making room
for the man whose words and actions
show that he knows where he is going.
-Napoleon Hill

291
There is no path to Happiness.
Happiness is the path.
There is no path to Love.
Love is the path.
There is no path to Peace.
Peace is the path.
-Dan Millman

292
We do not remember days.
We remember moments.
-Cesare Pavese

293
What you are afraid of
is never as bad as what you imagine.
The fear you let build up in your mind
is worse than the situation that actually exists.
-Spencer Johnson

294
People often say that motivation doesn't last.
Well, neither does bathing, that's why
we recommend it daily.
-Zig Ziglar

295
Holding on to anger is like grasping a hot coal
with the intent of throwing it at someone else;
you are the one who gets burned.
-Buddha

296
Believe in yourself, never give up,
and go about your business
with passion drive and enthusiasm.
-Peter Jones

297
Circumstances do not make a man,
they reveal him.
-James Allen

298
The more you see yourself as what you'd like to become, and act as if what you want is already there, the more you'll activate those dormant forces that will collaborate to transform your dream into your reality.
-Wayne Dyer

299
Feel the fear and do it anyway!
-Susan Jeffers

300
You only live once,
but if you do it right,
once is enough.
-Mae West

301
It's only possible to live happily ever after on a moment-to-moment basis.
-Margaret Bonnano

## 302
Every time you are tempted to react in the same
old way, ask if you want to be a prisoner of the
past or a pioneer of the future.
-Deepak Chopra

## 303
The secret of success in life
is for a man to be ready
for his opportunity when it comes.
-Benjamin Disraeli

## 304
The best day of your life
is the one on which you decide
your life is your own.
No apologies or excuses.
No one to lean on, rely on, or blame.
The gift is yours - it is an amazing journey -
and you alone are responsible for the quality of it.
This is the day that your life really begins.
-Bob Moawab

305
All our dreams can come true,
if we have the courage to pursue them.
-Walt Disney

306
At the end of the day,
let there be no excuses,
no explanations, no regrets.
-Steve Maraboli

307
Failure is simply the opportunity to begin again,
this time more intelligently.
-Henry Ford

308
And in the end, it's not the years in your life that
count. It's the life in your years.
-Abraham Lincoln

## 309
Efficiency is doing things right;
effectiveness is doing the right things.
-Peter Drucker

## 310
If you are never scared, embarrassed, or hurt,
it means you never take chances.
-Julia Soul

## 311
A diamond is merely a lump of coal
that did well under pressure.
-Unknown

# 312

So many of our dreams
at first seem impossible,
then they seem improbable,
and then,
when we summon the will,
they soon become inevitable.
-Christopher Reeve

313
We find comfort among those who agree with us,
growth among those who don't.
-Frank Clark


314
Your current life is the result of your previous
choices, if you want something different,
begin to choose differently.
-Joe Tichio


315
It is only with the heart that one can see rightly;
what is essential is invisible to the eye.
-Antoine de Saint-Exupery


316
Those who bring sunshine to the lives of others
cannot keep it from themselves.
-James Matthew Barrie

317
As you move toward a dream,
the dream moves toward you.
-Julia Cameron


318
The only people with whom you should try to get
even are those who have helped you.
-John E. Southard


319
Limitations live only in our minds.
But if we use our imaginations,
our possibilities become limitless.
-Jamie Paolinetti


320
If you have built castles in the air,
your work need not be lost.
That is where they should be.
Now put the foundation under them.
-Henry David Thoreau

### 321
This time like all times is a very good one
if we but know what to do with it.
-Ralph Waldo Emerson


### 322
Most people who fail in their dream
fail not from lack of ability,
but from lack of commitment.
-Zig Ziglar


### 323
Fear is not your enemy.
It is a compass pointing you
to the areas where you need to grow.
-Steve Pavlina


### 324
The only one who can tell you 'you can't' is you.
And you don't have to listen.
-Nike

325
Kites rise highest against the wind, not with it.
-Winston Churchill


326
We cannot change the cards we are dealt,
just how we play the hand.
-Randy Pausch


327
Worry never robs tomorrow of its sorrow,
it only saps today of its joy.
-Leo Buscaglia


328
Thinking will not overcome fear,
but action will.
-W. Clement Stone

329
One of the easiest ways to begin clarifying
what you truly want is to make a list of
30 things you want to do,
30 things you want to have,
and 30 things you want to be
before you die.
-Jack Canfield


330
The biggest mistake people make in life
is not trying to make a living
at doing what they enjoy most.
-Malcolm Forbes


331
You don't have to see the whole staircase,
just take the first step.
-Martin Luther King, Jr.

332
Without goals, and plans to reach them,
you are like a ship that has set sail
with no destination.
-Fitzhugh Dodson


333
As soon as you trust yourself,
you will know how to live.
-Goethe


334
The minute I stopped caring what other people
thought and started doing what I wanted to do
is the minute I finally felt free.
-Phil Dunphy


335
The place to improve the world
is first in one's own heart and head and hands,
and then work outward from there.
-Robert M. Pirsig

336
Do you really want to be happy?
You can begin by being appreciative of who you
are and what you've got.
-Benjamin Hoff

337
Two men looked out from prison bars,
one saw the mud, the other saw stars.
-Dale Carnegie

338
Insanity is doing the same thing,
over and over again,
but expecting different results.
-Albert Einstein

339
Stop saying 'I Wish'
and start saying 'I Will'.
-Unknown

340
You leave old habits behind
by starting out with the thought,
'I release the need for this in my life'.
-Wayne Dyer

341
Change is inevitable.
Growth is optional.
-John C. Maxwell

342
If you really want something, you'll find a way.
If you don't, you'll find an excuse.
-Unknown

343
It's not the load that breaks you down,
it's the way you carry it.
-Lou Holtz

344
What is the point of being alive
if you don't at least try
to do something remarkable?
-John Green


345
We are not held back by the love we didn't
receive in the past, but by the love we're not
extending in the present.
-Marianne Williamson


346
The only place where success comes before work
is in the dictionary.
-Donald M. Kendall


347
You can only lose something that you have,
you cannot lose something that you are.
-Eckhart Tolle

348

Everybody is a genius.
But if you judge a fish
by its ability to climb a tree,
it will live its whole life
believing that it is stupid.
-Unknown

349
If you go looking for a friend,
you're going to find they're very scarce.
If you go out to be a friend,
you'll find them everywhere.
-Zig Ziglar


350
Winning isn't everything,
but wanting to win is.
-Vince Lombardi


351
Man cannot discover new oceans
unless he has the courage
to lose sight of the shore.
-Andre Gide


352
Efforts and courage are not enough
without purpose and direction.
-John F. Kennedy

353
Too many people overvalue what they are not
and undervalue what they are.
-Malcolm S. Forbes

354
If one dream should fall and break into a thousand
pieces, never be afraid to pick one of those pieces
up and begin again.
-Flavia Weedn

355
Instead of giving myself reasons why I can't,
I give myself reasons why I can.
-Unknown

356
He who works with his hands is a laborer.
He who works with his
hands and his head is a craftsman.
He who works with his
hands and his head and his heart is an artist.
-St. Francis of Assisi

357
There is no passion to be found playing small -
in settling for a life that is less
than the one you are capable of living.
-Nelson Mandela


358
We change our behavior
when the pain of staying the same
becomes greater than the pain of changing.
Consequences give us the pain
that motivates us to change.
-Henry Cloud


359
And the day came
when the risk to remain tight in a bud
was more painful than the risk it took to blossom.
-Anais Nin

360
It is our choices that show what we truly are,
far more than our abilities.
-J.K. Rowling

361
It's a very funny thing about life;
if you refuse to accept anything but the best,
you very often get it.
-William Somerset Maugham

362
Life is made of millions of moments,
but we live only one of these moments at a time.
As we begin to change this moment,
we begin to change our lives.
-Trinidad Hunt

363
Yesterday is history.
Tomorrow is a mystery.
Today is a gift,
that's why it's called the Present.
-Unknown


364
Although time seems to fly by,
it never travels faster than one day at a time.
Each day is a new opportunity
to live your life to the fullest.
-Steve Maraboli


365
All is Well.
-Esther Hicks

# AFTERWORD

I hope you enjoyed this inspiring 365 day journey to more happiness, success, and motivation. It's been said we write the books we most need to read. Well, writing this book has been an incredible experience. For a few months I spent several hours each day surrounded by inspirational quotes, stories, and people. Little by little that inspiration dug its way into my core, set up camp, and has no plans of leaving.

"Slow and steady wins the race."

Most of us are pretty busy and we find ourselves short on time. I designed this book to easily fit into just about everyone's schedule. Reading just one quote a day takes a few seconds. If you carry it around and read the same quote several times throughout the day, you may spend at most 2 - 3 minutes. I feel that's something we can all easily make time for even in the busiest of lives.

Be like the tortoise in Aesop's fairy tale, *The Tortoise and the Hare*. Rather than racing hard and tiring yourself out, take it one step at a time, consistently moving in the right direction. Life is not a race, but if it was, the finish line is the same for all of us. Take it easy, keep moving in the direction you choose, and remember to have fun.

Enjoy your journey-- much love,
Dr. Joe Tichio

# FREE BONUS

Go to **www.Greatest-Inspirational-Quotes.com** and sign up for the Inspirational Quotes Newsletter. In addition to a monthly inspirational message, you will also receive a complimentary copy of the timeless classic *As a Man Thinketh* by James Allen.

# INDEX

9. **Jim Rohn**: entrepreneur, author, and motivational speaker. He developed programs to assist others to reach success in business and life. Learn more by visiting his website **www.jimrohn.com**

10. **Norman Cousins**: American journalist, author, professor, and world peace advocate.

11. **Franklin P. Jones**: reporter and humorist known for his column "Put it this Way" in the Saturday Evening Post. His column was the longest continuously published feature in the Saturday Evening Post.

12. **H. Jackson Brown, Jr**: author best known for his inspirational book, *The Complete Life's Little Instruction Book*. Learn more by visiting his website **www.instructionbook.com**

13. **Unknown**

14. **Ambrose Redmoon**: real name was James Neil Hollingworth. He was a beatnik writer and manager of the rock band Quicksilver Messenger Service.

15. **Hilary Hinton "Zig" Ziglar**: salesman, author, and motivational speaker. Zig Ziglar shared a philosophy of long-term, balanced success focusing on character, attitude, and skills. Learn more by visiting **www.ziglar.com**

16. **Anthony Robbins**: one of the biggest names in the self-help field. Robbins helps people transform the quality of their lives, become better leaders, and reach peak performance. To learn more visit his website **www.tonyrobbins.com**

17. **William B. Sprague**: clergyman and compiler of *Annals of the American Pulpit*. This quote has also been attributed to William Butler Yeats.

18. **Mary Engelbreit**: started her career creating greeting cards, which became very successful. She then became editor-in-chief of *Mary Engelbreit's Home Companion*, and eventually fulfilled her childhood dream of illustrating children's books. Learn more about her by visiting **www.maryengelbreit.com**

19. **Leo Buscaglia**: aka "Dr. Love" was an author, professor, and motivational speaker. His main message was to give more love, accept more love, and open your heart to life. His books include: *Living, Loving, and Learning, The Way of the Bull*, and *Personhood*. Learn more at **www.buscaglia.com**

20. **Harold Thurman**: philosopher, theologian, educator, and civil rights leader. He founded a multicultural church, wrote 21 books, and was Dean of Chapel at Howard University and Boston University.

21. **Dale Carnegie**: author of *How to Win Friends and Influence People*. He was a writer, lecturer, and developer of self-improvement courses. Learn more at **www.dalecarnegie.com**

22. **Claude Bissell**: Canadian author, educator, and eighth president of the University of Toronto.

23. **Nikki Giovanni**: currently a distinguished professor at Virginia Tech. She's also a poet, writer, commentator, and activist. Learn more by visiting **www.nikki-giovanni.com**

24. **Unknown**

25. **Ralph Waldo Emerson**: American essayist, lecturer, and poet who led the Transcendentalist movement in the mid 19$^{th}$ century. He is most famous for *Self-Reliance, The American Scholar*, and *Nature*.

26. **Jim Rohn**: entrepreneur, author, and motivational speaker. He developed programs to assist others to reach success in business and life. Learn more by visiting his website **www.jimrohn.com**

27. **John Lennon**: English musician, singer, songwriter, and one of the founding members of the Beatles. Learn more by visiting **www.johnlennon.com**

28. **Pope Paul VI**: born Giovanni Battista Enrico Antonio Maria Montini. Pope of the Roman Catholic Church from June 21, 1963 - August 6, 1978.

29. **James Allen**: British philosophical writer known for his inspirational books and poetry. His most famous book, *As a Man Thinketh*, has been a major source of inspiration for self-help authors. As a bonus, you may get a free copy of *As a Man Thinketh* by visiting **www.Greatest-Inspirational-Quotes.com**

30. **Kahlil Gibran**: Lebanese-American artist, writer, and poet. He's most famous for his 1923 book *The Prophet*.

31. **Hilary Hinton "Zig" Ziglar**: salesman, author, and motivational speaker. Zig Ziglar shared a philosophy of long-term, balanced success focusing on character, attitude, and skills. Learn more by visiting **www.ziglar.com**

32. **Ralph Waldo Emerson**: American essayist, lecturer, and poet who led the Transcendentalist movement in the mid 19th century. He is most famous for *Self-Reliance*, *The American Scholar*, and *Nature*.

33. **Admiral William Halsey Jr**: United States Naval officer who commanded the South Pacific Area during the early stages of the Pacific War.

34. **Uta Hagen**: American actress and highly influential acting teacher, who originated the role of Martha in the 1963 premiere of *Who's Afraid of Virginia Woolf* by Edward Albee.

35. **Father Alfred D'Souza**: inspirational writer and philosopher from Brisbane, Australia who died in 2004. He's often referred to as Father Alfred D. Souza.

36. **Dale Carnegie**: author of *How to Win Friends and Influence People*. He was a writer, lecturer, and developer of self-improvement courses. Learn more at **www.dalecarnegie.com**

37. **Seneca**: major philosophical figure of the Roman Imperial Period.

38. **Angelina Jolie**: American actress, director, Academy Award winner, and one of Hollywood's highest paid actresses. She promotes humanitarian causes and is a former Goodwill Ambassador for the United Nations.

39. **Buckminster "Bucky" Fuller**: American systems theorist, engineer, author, architect, designer, inventor, and futurist. Learn more by visiting the Buckminster Fuller Institute at **www.bfi.org**

40. **Vince Lombardi**: best known as the head coach of the Green Bay Packers during the 1960s. He led them to victory in the first two Super Bowls. Learn more by visiting **www.vincelombardi.com**

41. **Diane Ackerman**: American author, poet, and naturalist best known for her work *A Natural History of the Senses*. Learn more by visiting **www.dianeackerman.com**

42. **Steve Pavlina**: American self-help author, speaker, and creator of the very successful blog **www.stevepavlina.com**

43. **Eleanor Roosevelt**: wife of President Franklin D. Roosevelt. She was an advocate for civil rights, an international author, speaker, and politician.
44. **Unknown**
45. **C.S. Lewis**: author of *The Chronicles of Narnia*. Learn more by visiting **www.cslewis.com**
46. **Hugh Downs**: American broadcaster, television host, news anchor, and author.
47. **Ralph Waldo Emerson**: American essayist, lecturer, and poet who led the Transcendentalist movement in the mid 19$^{th}$ century. He is most famous for *Self-Reliance*, *The American Scholar*, and *Nature*.
48. **Katharine Hepburn**: four-time Academy Award winning actress, famous for her independent and spirited personality.
49. **Ella Fitzgerald**: dubbed "The First Lady of Song", she was the most popular female jazz singer in the United States. Learn more by visiting **www.ellafitzgerald.com**
50. **Anais Nin**: French-Cuban author best known for her life and times in *The Diary of Anais Nin*, Vols. I-VII. Learn more by visiting **www.anaisnin.com**
51. **Thomas A. Edison**: American inventor and businessman. He developed the phonograph, motion picture camera, and the light bulb.
52. **Johann Wolfgang von Goethe**: German writer, artist, and politician.
53. **Anthony Robbins**: one of the biggest names in the self-help field. Robbins helps people transform the quality of their lives, become better leaders, and reach peak performance. To learn more visit his website **www.tonyrobbins.com**
54. **Unknown**

55. **Cavett Robert**: He established the National Speaker's Association (NSA) and founded it on the premise that helping others is our most noble attribute. Learn more at **www.cavettrobert.com**

56. **Richard Bach**: American writer most famous for his bestselling books *Jonathan Livingston Seagull* and *Illusions: The Adventures of a Reluctant Messiah*. Learn more at **www.richardbach.com**

57. **Henry David Thoreau**: American author, poet, philosopher, and leading transcendentalist. He is best known for his book *Walden* and essay *Civil Disobedience*.

58. **Joshua J. Marine**: I've come across this quote in several places attributing it to Joshua J. Marine, but unfortunately I could not find any reliable information about this person.

59. **Dan Millman**: American author and speaker, most famous for his book, *Way of The Peaceful Warrior*. Learn more by visiting **www.peacefulwarrior.com**

60. **Helen Keller**: contracted a disease at 19 months old, which left her deaf and blind. With the help of Anne Sullivan she managed to become an author, political activist, and lecturer.

61. **Thomas J. Watson**: chairman and CEO of IBM from 1914 - 1956. He was a self-made industrialist and one of the richest men of his time.

62. **Hilary Hinton "Zig" Ziglar**: salesman, author, and motivational speaker. Zig Ziglar shared a philosophy of long-term, balanced success focusing on character, attitude, and skills. Learn more by visiting **www.ziglar.com**

63. **Epictetus**: Greek sage and Stoic philosopher from AD 55 - AD 135.

64. **Ken S. Keyes, Jr**: personal growth author, lecturer, and developed the Living Love method of self-help.

65. **Joan Baez**: American folk singer, songwriter, musician, and activist for human rights, peace, and environmental justice. Learn more at **www.joanbaez.com**

66. **Leon C. Megginson**: management sociologist paraphrasing Charles Darwin.

67. **Brian Tracy**: self-help author, motivational speaker, and business coach. Learn more at **www.briantracy.com**

68. **Jason Fried and David Heinemeier Hansson**: Jason Fried is the co-founder and president of 37signals. David Heinemeier Hansson is a partner at 37 signals. Together they co-wrote the book *Rework*. Learn more about them at **www.37signals.com**

69. **Wayne Dyer**: American self-help author and motivational speaker. Learn more at **www.drwaynedyer.com**

70. **Vesta Kelly**: I've come across this quote in several places attributing it to Vesta Kelly, but unfortunately I could not find any reliable information about this person.

71. **Steve Jobs**: American entrepreneur best known as the co-founder, chairman, and CEO of Apple Inc.

72. **Albert Schweitzer**: German theologian, organist, philosopher, physician, and medical missionary. In 1952, he received the Nobel Peace Prize for his philosophy of "Reverence for Life".

73. **Friedrich Nietzsche**: German philosopher, poet, composer, and cultural critic.

74. **Lewis Cass**: American military officer and politician.

75. **Joseph Chilton Pearce**: American author of books on child development.

76. **Benjamin Spock**: American pediatrician famous for his book, *Baby and Child Care*, published in 1946 and one of the best-sellers of all time.

77. **Jim Rohn**: entrepreneur, author, and motivational speaker. He developed programs to assist others to reach success in business and life. Learn more by visiting his website **www.jimrohn.com**

78. **Bethany Hamilton**: American professional surfer famous for surviving a shark attack in which her left arm was bitten off. Read more at **www.bethanyhamilton.com**

79. **George Bernard Shaw**: Irish playwright, essayist, novelist, and co-founder of the London School of Economics.

80. **Michael Jordan**: considered by many to be the greatest basketball player of all time.

81. **Confucius**: Chinese teacher, editor, politician, and philosopher from 551–479 BC.

82. **Randy Pausch**: American professor of computer science and human-computer interaction. Before passing away of pancreatic cancer, he gave an upbeat lecture titled "The Last Lecture: Really Achieving Your Childhood Dreams". Read more at **www.thelastlecture.com**

83. **Bobby McFerrin**: 10 Grammy Award winning American vocalist and conductor best known for his hit song "Don't Worry, Be Happy". Learn more at **www.bobbymcferrin.com**

84. **James F. Byrnes**: American politician from the state of South Carolina.

85. **Unknown**

86. **Audre Lorde**: Caribbean-American writer, poet, and activist.

87. **Maya Angelou**: American author and poet. Her most famous book is *I Know Why the Caged Bird Sings*. Learn more at **www.mayaangelou.com**

88. **Pablo Picasso**: Spanish painter, sculptor, printmaker, ceramicist, and stage designer. Considered one of the greatest and most influential artists of the 20<sup>th</sup> century.

89. **Sandra Carey**: I've come across this quote in several places attributing it to Sandra Carey, but unfortunately I could not find any reliable information about this person.

90. **W. Clement Stone**: businessman, philanthropist, and self-help author.

91. **Albert Szent-Györgyi**: Hungarian physiologist who won the Nobel Prize in Physiology or Medicine in 1937 and credited for discovering Vitamin C.

92. **Anna Quindlen**: American author, journalist, and opinion columnist, whose New York Times column, Public and Private, won the Pulitzer Prize for Commentary in 1992.

93. **Cypher Raige**: character from the movie *After Earth*, played by Will Smith.

94. **H. Jackson Brown, Jr**: author best known for his inspirational book, *The Complete Life's Little Instruction Book*. Learn more by visiting his website **www.instructionbook.com**

95. **Aurora Greenway**: character from *Terms of Endearment*, played by Shirley MacLaine. The original novel was written by Larry McMurty and adapted for film by James L. Brooks.

96. **Mary Pickford**: Canadian-American motion picture actress known as "America's Sweetheart", she was a significant figure in the development of film acting.

97. **Ayn Rand**: Russian-American novelist, philosopher, playwright, and screenwriter. She is best known for her novels *The Fountainhead* and *Atlas Shrugged* and developing the philosophical system called Objectivism.

98. **Roger Miller**: American singer, songwriter, musician, and actor.

99. **Winston Churchill**: British politician best known for his leadership of the United Kingdom during the Second World War.

100. **Mahatma Gandhi**: preeminent leader of Indian nationalism in British-ruled India, employing non-violent civil disobedience. He led India to independence and inspired movements for non-violence, civil rights, and freedom across the world.

101. **Alfred North Whitehead**: English mathematician and philosopher. He supervised the doctoral dissertation of Bertrand Russell and co-authored the epochal *Principia Mathematica* with Russell.

102. **Anatole France**: French poet, journalist, and novelist who won the Nobel Prize for Literature.

103. **Lloyd Jones**: I've come across this quote in several places attributing it to author Lloyd Jones, but unfortunately I could not find any reliable information about this person.

104. **John Wooden**: American basketball player and coach, nicknamed the "Wizard of Westwood". He was the first person to be inducted into the Basketball Hall of Fame as both a player and a coach. Learn more at **www.coachwooden.com**

105. **Buddha**: spiritual teacher from the Indian subcontinent, on whose teachings Buddhism was founded.

106. **Dolly Parton**: country singer-songwriter, musician, actress, author, and philanthropist. Read more at **www.dollyparton.com**

107. **Eleanor Roosevelt**: wife of President Franklin D. Roosevelt. She was an advocate for civil rights, an international author, speaker, and politician.

108. **Aldous Huxley**: English writer best known for his novel *Brave New World*.

109. **George Carlin**: five time Grammy Award winning comedian, social critic, actor, and writer/author. Learn more at **www.georgecarlin.com**

110. **Francis Chan**: American preacher and author of the bestselling book, *Crazy Love, Overwhelmed by a Restless God*. Visit his website to learn more **www.francischan.org**

111. **Seneca**: major philosophical figure of the Roman Imperial Period.

112. **Wayne Dyer**: American self-help author and motivational speaker. Learn more at **www.drwaynedyer.com**

113. **Anthony Robbins**: one of the biggest names in the self-help field. Robbins helps people transform the quality of their lives, become better leaders, and reach peak performance. To learn more visit his website **www.tonyrobbins.com**

114. **Robert Louis Stevenson**: Scottish novelist, poet, essayist, and travel writer. His most famous works are *Treasure Island* and *The Strange Case of Dr. Jekyll and Mr. Hyde*.

115. **Oprah Winfrey**: most famous for her self-titled talk show, which was the highest rated of its kind in history. In the mid 1990s, she refocused her show from tabloid style to an emphasis on literature, self improvement, and spirituality. Find out more by visiting **www.oprah.com**

116. **Elizabeth Kenny**: Australian nurse whose controversial treatment of poliomyelitis became the foundation of physical therapy.

117. **Dale Carnegie**: author of *How to Win Friends and Influence People*. He was a writer, lecturer, and developer of self-improvement courses. Learn more at **www.dalecarnegie.com**

118. **Henry David Thoreau**: American author, poet, philosopher, and leading transcendentalist. He is best known for his book *Walden* and essay *Civil Disobedience.*

119. **Patti Digh**: author of six bestsellers including *Life is a Verb.* Learn more by visiting her website **www.37days.com**

120. **Aristotle**: Greek philosopher, student of Plato, and teacher of Alexander the Great.

121. **Unknown**

122. **H. Jackson Brown, Jr**: author best known for his inspirational book, *The Complete Life's Little Instruction Book.* Learn more by visiting his website **www.instructionbook.com**

123. **Unknown**

124. **Robert Allen**: Canadian-American businessman and author, most famous for co-authoring the book *The One Minute Millionaire.* Learn more at **www.robertgallen.com**

125. **Osho**: Indian mystic, guru, and spiritual teacher with an international following. Learn more by visiting **www.osho.com**

126. **Francesca Reigler**: I've come across this quote in several places attributing it to Francesca Reigler, but unfortunately I could not find any reliable information about this person.

127. **Unknown**

128. **Les Brown**: top motivational speaker, speech coach, and bestselling author. Learn more at his website **www.lesbrown.org**

129. **Oprah Winfrey**: most famous for her self-titled talk show, which was the highest rated of its kind in history. In the mid 1990s, she refocused her show from tabloid style to an emphasis on literature, self improvement, and spirituality. Find out more by visiting **www.oprah.com**

130. **James Cook**: British explorer, navigator, and captain in the Royal Navy.

131. **Unknown**

132. **Martin Luther King, Jr**: American clergyman, activist, and prominent leader in the Civil Rights Movement.

133. **D.T. Suzuki**: Japanese author of books and essays on Buddhism, Zen, and Shin that were instrumental in spreading these concepts to the West.

134. **Lao Tzu**: philosopher of ancient China and best known as the author of the Tao Te Ching, a fundamental text of Taoism.

135. **Unknown**

136. **Terence**: aka Publius Terentius Afer, was an ancient Roman playwright (195 -159 BC).

137. **Spencer Johnson**: author of *Who Moved My Cheese? An Amazing Way to Deal with Change in Your Work and in Your Life*.
138. **Mike Ditka**: former American football player, commentator, and most famous for being head coach of the Chicago Bears. Learn more at **www.mikeditka.com**
139. **Les Brown**: top motivational speaker, speech coach, and best-selling author. Learn more at his website **www.lesbrown.org**
140. **Maureen Dowd**: American columnist for The New York Times, best-selling author, and Pulitzer Prize winner.
141. **Unknown**
142. **Mantak Chia**: Taoist master from Thailand, author, and teacher whose focus is to help his students empower themselves through the cultivation of their qi.
143. **George Bernard Shaw**: Irish playwright, essayist, novelist, and co-founder of the London School of Economics.
144. **William Blake**: English poet, painter, and printmaker. He is considered a seminal figure in the history of both the poetry and visual arts of the Romantic Age.
145. **Unknown**
146. **Carlos Castaneda**: was a Peruvian-American author, most famous for his series of books, *The Teachings of Don Juan*.
147. **Robert Allen**: Canadian-American businessman and author, most famous for co-authoring the book *The One Minute Millionaire*. Learn more at **www.robertgallen.com**
148. **Unknown**

149. **John Lennon**: English musician, singer, songwriter, and one of the founding members of the Beatles. Learn more by visiting **www.johnlennon.com**

150. **Grace Hansen**: I've come across this quote in several places attributing it to Grace Hansen, but unfortunately I could not find any reliable information about this person.

151. **William James**: American philosopher, psychologist, and author. He was the first educator to offer a psychology course in the United States.

152. **Harriet Beecher Stowe**: American abolitionist and author. Her novel *Uncle Tom's Cabin* was influential to the anti-slavery forces in the North and provoked anger in the South.

153. **Wayne Dyer**: American self-help author and motivational speaker. Learn more at **www.drwaynedyer.com**

154. **John Mason**: best-selling author, minister, and speaker. Learn more at his website **www.freshword.com**

155. **Elisabeth Kubler-Ross**: Swiss American psychiatrist, educator, and author of the groundbreaking book *On Death and Dying*.

156. **Lois Hurst**: I've come across this quote in several places attributing it to Lois Hurst, but unfortunately I could not find any reliable information about this person.

157. **Confucius**: Chinese teacher, editor, politician, and philosopher.

158. **Richard Bach**: American writer most famous for his bestselling books *Jonathan Livingston Seagull* and *Illusions: The Adventures of a Reluctant Messiah*. Learn more at **www.richardbach.com**

159. **Margaret B. Runbeck**: American author.

160. **Proverb**
161. **Albert Einstein**: regarded as the father of modern physics and the most influential physicist of the 20$^{th}$ century.
162. **Leo Buscaglia**: aka "Dr. Love" was an author, professor, and motivational speaker. His main message was to give more love, accept more love, and open your heart to life. His books include: *Living, Loving, and Learning, The Way of the Bull*, and *Personhood*. Learn more at **www.buscaglia.com**
163. **Judy Garland**: American actress, singer, and vaudevillian.
164. **Jim Rohn**: entrepreneur, author, and motivational speaker. He developed programs to assist others to reach success in business and life. Learn more by visiting his website **www.jimrohn.com**
165. **Epictetus**: Greek sage and Stoic philosopher from AD 55 - AD 135.
166. **David Weatherford**: child psychologist and writer. Learn more at **www.davidlweatherford.com**
167. **Mary Kay Ash**: American businesswoman and founder of Mary Kay Cosmetics.
168. **Henry Van Dyke**: American author, educator, and clergyman.
169. **Lucille Ball**: American comedian, actress, and star of *I Love Lucy*.
170. **Unknown**
171. **Edwin Elliot**: English poet.
172. **Napoleon Hill**: author of *Think and Grow Rich*, one of the best-selling books of all time. Find out more at **www.naphill.org**

173. **Nike**: American corporation developing and selling athletic footwear, apparel, equipment, and accessories.

174. **Richard Bach**: American writer most famous for his bestselling books *Jonathan Livingston Seagull* and *Illusions: The Adventures of a Reluctant Messiah*. Learn more at **www.richardbach.com**

175. **Dr. Seuss**: real name was Theodor Seuss Geisel. He was an American poet, writer, and cartoonist famous for the Dr. Seuss children's books.

176. **Steve Jobs**: American entrepreneur best known as the co-founder, chairman, and CEO of Apple, Inc.

177. **Joe Tichio**: author of this book, chiropractor, and creator of **www.Greatest-Inspirational-Quotes.com**

178. **Ralph Waldo Emerson**: American essayist, lecturer, and poet who led the Transcendentalist movement in the mid 19$^{th}$ century. He is most famous for *Self-Reliance*, *The American Scholar*, and *Nature*.

179. **Bob Marley**: Jamaican singer-songwriter and musician. He is the most widely known performer of reggae music worldwide.

180. **Winston Churchill**: British politician best known for his leadership of the United Kingdom during the Second World War.

181. **Albert Einstein**: regarded as the father of modern physics and the most influential physicist of the 20$^{th}$ century.

182. **Bruce Lee**: actor, martial artist, and philosopher. He is widely considered to be one of the most influential martial artists of all time.

183. **Jim Rohn**: entrepreneur, author, and motivational speaker. He developed programs to assist others to reach success in business and life. Learn more by visiting his website **www.jimrohn.com**

184. **Leigh Hunt**: full name was James Henry Leigh Hunt an English critic, essayist, and poet.

185. **Donald Kaufman**: character from the movie Adaptation played by Nicolas Cage. The book was written by Susan Orlean and adapted for film by Charlie Kaufman.

186. **Stephen Covey**: American educator, author, speaker, and businessman. His most popular book was *The Seven Habits of Highly Effective People*. Learn more at **www.stephencovey.com**

187. **Oscar Wilde**: Irish writer, poet, and playwright. His most famous work was *The Important of Being Earnest*.

188. **Oliver Wendell Holmes**: American physician, poet, professor, and author. His most famous prose works are the *Breakfast-Table* series.

189. **Doe Zantamata**: author of *Happiness in Your Life*, learn more at **www.happinessinyourlife.com**

190. **Babe Ruth**: George Herman Ruth, Jr., aka Babe, the Bambino, and the Sultan of Swat. He was an American baseball player and elected into the National Baseball Hall of Fame.

191. **Peter Ralston**: American martial artist and the first non-Asian to win the full-contact World Championships held in China. Also, an author and teacher of a dogma free approach to consciousness. Learn more at **www.chenghsin.com**

192. **Norman Vincent Peale**: minister, proponent of positive thinking, and author of *The Power of Positive Thinking*.

193. **Charles Farmer**: character played by Billy Bob Thornton in the *Astronaut Farmer*, written by Mark Polish and Michael Polish.

194. **Admiral William Halsey Jr**: United States Naval officer who commanded the South Pacific Area during the early stages of the Pacific War.

195. **Will Smith**: American actor, producer, and rapper.

196. **Leo Buscaglia**: aka "Dr. Love" was an author, professor, and motivational speaker. His main message was to give more love, accept more love, and open your heart to life. His books include: *Living, Loving, and Learning*, *The Way of the Bull*, and *Personhood*. Learn more at **www.buscaglia.com**

197. **Steve Pavlina**: American self-help author, speaker, and creator of the very successful blog, **www.stevepavlina.com**

198. **Hilary Hinton "Zig" Ziglar**: salesman, author, and motivational speaker. Zig Ziglar shared a philosophy of long-term, balanced success focusing on character, attitude, and skills. Learn more by visiting **www.ziglar.com**

199. **Patch Adams**: American physician, social activist, clown, and author. Learn more about his work at **www.patchadams.org**

200. **Virgil**: Publius Vergilius Maro was an ancient Roman poet and traditionally ranked as one of Rome's greatest poets.

201. **Dr. Joyce Brothers**: American psychologist, television personality, and advice columnist.

202. **Abraham Lincoln**: 16th president of the United States and led the country through the American Civil War.
203. **Anthony Robbins**: one of the biggest names in the self help field. Robbins helps people transform the quality of their lives, become better leaders, and reach peak performance. To learn more visit his website **www.tonyrobbins.com**
204. **Unknown**
205. **Unknown**
206. **Aristotle**: Greek philosopher, student of Plato, and teacher of Alexander the Great.
207. **Lao Tzu**: philosopher of ancient China and best known as the author of the Tao Te Ching, a fundamental text of Taoism.
208. **Neale Donald Walsch**: author of the series *Conversations with God*. Learn more by visiting his website **www.nealedonaldwalsch.com**
209. **Andre Gide**: French author and winner of the Nobel Prize in literature in 1947.
210. **Soren Kierkegaard**: Danish philosopher, theologian, poet, social critic, and religious author. He is widely considered to be the first existential philosopher.
211. **Jim Rohn**: entrepreneur, author, and motivational speaker. He developed programs to assist others to reach success in business and life. Learn more by visiting his website **www.jimrohn.com**
212. **Bruce Lee**: actor, martial artist, and philosopher. He is widely considered to be one of the most influential martial artists of all time.
213. **Joe Tichio**: author of this book, chiropractor, and creator of **www.Greatest-Inspirational-Quotes.com**

214. **Eckhart Tolle**: best known as the author of *The Power of Now* and *A New Earth*. Learn more at **www.eckharttolletv.com**

215. **Robert Brault**: free-lance writer who has contributed to magazines and newspapers in the United States for over 40 years. His famous quote is sometimes mistakenly attributed to Kurt Vonnegut. Learn more at **www.robertbrault.com**

216. **Unknown**

217. **Virginia Satir**: widely regarded as the "Mother of Family Therapy", she was an American author and psychotherapist known for her approach to family therapy. Learn more by visiting **www.satirinstitute.org**

218. **Dr. Seuss**: his real name was Theodor Seuss Geisel. He was an American poet, writer, and cartoonist famous for the Dr. Seuss children's books.

219. **Leo Buscaglia**: aka "Dr. Love" was an author, professor, and motivational speaker. His main message was to give more love, accept more love, and open your heart to life. His books include: *Living, Loving, and Learning*, *The Way of the Bull*, and *Personhood*. Learn more at **www.buscaglia.com**

220. **Unknown**

221. **Stephen Covey**: American educator, author, speaker, and businessman. His most popular book was *The Seven Habits of Highly Effective People*.

222. **Jed McKenna**: author of The Enlightenment Trilogy.

223. **Paulo Coelho**: Brazilian author, most famous for his book *The Alchemist*.

224. **Seth Godin**: American entrepreneur, author, and speaker. Learn more at **www.sethgodin.com**

225. **Matsuo Basho**: the most famous poet of the Edo period in Japan and widely recognized as the greatest master of haiku.
226. **Danny Kaye**: American actor, singer, dancer, and comedian.
227. **George Eliot**: Mary Anne Evans used the pen name George Eliot. She was an English novelist, journalist, and leading writer of the Victorian era.
228. **W. Clement Stone**: businessman, philanthropist, and self-help author.
229. **Albert Schweitzer**: German theologian, organist, philosopher, physician, and medical missionary. In 1952, he received the Nobel Peace Prize for his philosophy of "Reverence for Life".
230. **Charles Swindoll**: evangelical Christian pastor, author, and educator. Learn more by visiting **www.insight.org**.
231. **Sydney J. Harris**: journalist in Chicago, most famous for his column "Strictly Personal".
232. **Mary Jean Irion**: her last name is often incorrectly spelled Iron. This quote is a paragraph in her essay, "Let Me Hold You While I May" from the book *Yes, World*.
233. **Paulo Coelho**: Brazilian author, most famous for his book *The Alchemist*.
234. **Bruce Lee**: actor, martial artist, and philosopher. He is widely considered to be one of the most influential martial artists of all time.
235. **Mark Twain**: his real name was Samuel Langhorne Clemens. He was an American author and humorist best known for his novels *The Adventures of Tom Sawyer* and *Adventures of Huckleberry Finn*.

236. **Bernie Siegel**: American author and retired pediatric surgeon. He is known for his best-selling book *Love, Medicine, and Miracles*. Learn more at **www.berniesiegelmd.com**
237. **Thomas Carlyle**: Scottish writer, essayist, and historian during the Victorian era.
238. **Jim Rohn**: entrepreneur, author, and motivational speaker. He developed programs to assist others to reach success in business and life. Learn more by visiting his website **www.jimrohn.com**
239. **Barbara De Angelis**: American relationship consultant, author, and TV personality. Learn more at **www.barbaradeangelis.com**
240. **Tallulah Bankhead**: American actress and talk show host.
241. **Billy Wilder**: Austrian-born filmmaker, screenwriter, artist, and journalist. He was the writer and director of *The Apartment, Double Indemnity,* and *Sunset Boulevard.*
242. **Forest E. Witcraft**: scholar, teacher, and Boy Scout administrator. His quote sometimes ends with *the life of a boy-* instead of child.
243. **Unknown**
244. **Kahlil Gibran**: Lebanese-American artist, writer, and poet. He's most famous for his 1923 book *The Prophet.*
245. **Henry Ford**: American industrialist and founder of the Ford Motor Company.
246. **Richard Carlson**: American author, psychotherapist, and motivational speaker who rose to fame with the success of his book *Don't Sweat the Small Stuff...and it's all Small Stuff.*

247. **Hermann Hesse**: German-Swiss poet, novelist, and painter. His best known works are *Siddhartha* and *The Glass Bead Game*, each of which explores a person's search for an authentic life and self-knowledge. He received the Nobel Prize in Literature.

248. **Woody Allen**: American screenwriter, director, actor, and comedian.

249. **Christopher McDougall**: American author and journalist best known for his bestselling book *Born to Run*. Learn more at **www.chrismcdougall.com**

250. **Stephen Covey**: American educator, author, speaker, and businessman. His most popular book was *The Seven Habits of Highly Effective People*.

251. **Jason Fried and David Heinemeier Hansson**: Jason Fried is the co-founder and president of 37signals. David Heinemeier Hansson is a partner at 37 signals. Together they co-wrote the book *Rework*. Learn more about them at **www.37signals.com**

252. **Randy Pausch**: American professor of computer science and human-computer interaction. Before passing away of pancreatic cancer, he gave an upbeat lecture titled "The Last Lecture: Really Achieving Your Childhood Dreams". Read more at **www.thelastlecture.com**

253. **Augustine "Og" Mandino**: American author who wrote the best-selling book *The Greatest Salesman in the World*. Learn more by visiting **www.ogmandino.com**

254. **Arthur Koestler**: Hungarian-British author and journalist.

255. **Edward Estlin (E.E.) Cummings**: American poet, painter, author, and playwright.

256. **Proverb**

257. **Socrates**: classical Greek Athenian philosopher and teacher of Plato.

258. **Unknown**

259. **Shakti Gawain**: author known for her book *Creative Visualization*. Learn more at **www.shaktigawain.com**

260. **Dale Carnegie**: author of *How to Win Friends and Influence People*. He was a writer, lecturer, and developer of self-improvement courses. Learn more at **www.dalecarnegie.com**

261. **Ralph Waldo Emerson**: American essayist, lecturer, and poet who led the Transcendentalist movement in the mid 19th century. He is most famous for *Self-Reliance*, *The American Scholar*, and *Nature*.

262. **Anthony Robbins**: one of the biggest names in the self help field. Robbins helps people transform the quality of their lives, become better leaders, and reach peak performance. To learn more visit his website **www.tonyrobbins.com**

263. **Spencer Johnson**: author of *Who Moved My Cheese? An Amazing Way to Deal with Change in Your Work and in Your Life*.

264. **Florence Scovel Shinn**: artist and illustrator who later became a New Thought spiritual teacher. She is most famous for the book *The Game of Life and How to Play It*.

265. **Richard L. Evan**: member of the Quorum of the Twelve Apostles, President of Rotary International, and the writer, producer, and announcer of Music and the Spoken Word.

266. **Gretchen Rubin**: American author and blogger most famous for her book *The Happiness Project*. Learn more at her website **www.happiness-project.com**

267. **Winston Churchill**: British politician best known for his leadership of the United Kingdom during the Second World War.

268. **Paulo Coelho**: Brazilian author, most famous for his book *The Alchemist*.

269. **Warren Beatty**: American actor, producer, screenwriter, and director.

270. **Mark Twain**: his real name was Samuel Langhorne Clemens. He was an American author and humorist best known for his novels *The Adventures of Tom Sawyer* and *Adventures of Huckleberry Finn*.

271. **Jim Rohn**: entrepreneur, author, and motivational speaker. He developed programs to assist others to reach success in business and life. Learn more by visiting his website **www.jimrohn.com**

272. **Benjamin Disraeli**: British Prime Minister and statesman.

273. **Unknown**

274. **Unknown**

275. **Unknown**

276. **Proverb**

277. **Peter Ralston**: American martial artist and the first non-Asian to win the full-contact World Championships held in China. Also, an author and teacher of a dogma free approach to consciousness. Learn more at **www.chenghsin.com**

278. **Unknown**

279. **Randy Pausch**: American professor of computer science and human-computer interaction. Before passing away of pancreatic cancer, he gave an upbeat lecture titled "The Last Lecture: Really Achieving Your Childhood Dreams". Read more at **www.thelastlecture.com**

280. **Robert Louis Stevenson**: Scottish novelist, poet, essayist, and travel writer. His most famous works are *Treasure Island* and *Strange Case of Dr. Jekyll and Mr. Hyde.*

281. **John D. Rockefeller**: American industrialist, philanthropist, and founder of the Standard Oil Company. Adjusting for inflation, he is often regarded as the richest person in history.

282. **Pearl S. Buck**: American author, Pulitzer Prize winner, and awarded the Nobel Prize in Literature.

283. **Wayne Dyer**: American self-help author and motivational speaker. Learn more at **www.drwaynedyer.com**

284. **Jake Steinfeld**: American fitness personality famous for his line of equipment called "Body by Jake".

285. **Unknown**

286. **Frank Clark**: author of a column called "The Country Parson" for the Des Moines Register. His collections of quotes were compiled into small books.

287. **Unknown**

288. **Mitch Albom**: most famous for his best-selling books *Tuesdays with Morrie* and *The Five People You Meet in Heaven.* Learn more at **www.mitchalbom.com**

289. **Beverly Sills**: American operatic soprano.

290. **Napoleon Hill**: author of *Think and Grow Rich*, one of the bestselling books of all time. Find out more at **www.naphill.org**

291. **Dan Millman**: American author and speaker most famous for his book *Way of The Peaceful Warrior*. Learn more by visiting **www.peacefulwarrior.com**

292. **Cesare Pavese**: Italian poet, novelist, and literary critic.

293. **Spencer Johnson**: author of *Who Moved My Cheese? An Amazing Way to Deal with Change in Your Work and in Your Life*.

294. **Hilary Hinton "Zig" Ziglar**: salesman, author, and motivational speaker. Zig Ziglar shared a philosophy of long-term, balanced success focusing on character, attitude, and skills. Learn more by visiting **www.ziglar.com**

295. **Buddha**: was a spiritual teacher from the Indian subcontinent, on whose teachings Buddhism was founded.

296. **Peter Jones**: British entrepreneur and television personality with appearances on British television.

297. **James Allen**: British philosophical writer known for his inspirational books and poetry. His most famous book, *As a Man Thinketh*, has been a major source of inspiration for self-help authors. As a bonus, you may get a free copy of *As a Man Thinketh* by visiting **www.Greatest-Inspirational-Quotes.com**

298. **Wayne Dyer**: American self-help author and motivational speaker. Learn more at **www.drwaynedyer.com**

299. **Susan Jeffers**: author of the book *Feel the Fear and Do It Anyway*. Learn more at **www.susanjeffers.com**

300. **Mae West**: American actress, screenwriter, and sex symbol.
301. **Margaret Bonnano**: American science fiction writer (including six Star Trek novels) and small press publisher. Learn more at **www.margaretwanderbonanno.com**
302. **Deepak Chopra**: Indian-American physician, and holistic health/alternative medicine practitioner. Learn more at **www.deepakchopra.com**
303. **Benjamin Disraeli**: British Prime Minister and statesman.
304. **Bob Moawab**: American self-help author.
305. **Walt Disney**: American film producer, director, and animator. The Academy Awards gave him more awards and nominations than any other individual in history. Construction on Walt Disney World Resort in Florida began the year after he died.
306. **Steve Maraboli**: speaker and author on topics including inspiration, peak performance, and human potential. Learn more at **www.stevemaraboli.com**
307. **Henry Ford**: American industrialist, and founder of the Ford Motor Company.
308. **Abraham Lincoln**: 16th president of the United States and led the country through the American Civil War.
309. **Peter Drucker**: Austrian-born American management consultant, educator, and author.
310. **Julia Soul**: American actress.
311. **Unknown**
312. **Christopher Reeve**: American author, director, and actor most famous for playing Superman.

313. **Frank Clark**: author of a column called "The Country Parson" for the Des Moines Register. His collection of quotes were compiled into small books.
314. **Joe Tichio**: author of this book, chiropractor, and creator of **www.greatest-Inspirational-Quotes.com**
315. **Antoine de Saint-Exupéry**: French aristocrat, writer, and poet.
316. **James Matthew Barrie**: Scottish author and dramatist best remembered today as the creator of Peter Pan.
317. **Julia Cameron**: author of *The Artist's Way*. Learn more at **www.juliacameronlive.com**
318. **John E. Southard**: I've come across this quote in several places attributing it to John E. Southard, but unfortunately I could not find any reliable information about this person.
319. **Jamie Paolinetti**: bicycle racer, filmmaker, and writer.
320. **Henry David Thoreau**: American author, poet, philosopher, and leading transcendentalist. He is best known for his book *Walden* and essay *Civil Disobedience.*
321. **Ralph Waldo Emerson**: American essayist, lecturer, and poet who led the Transcendentalist movement in the mid 19th century. He is most famous for *Self-Reliance*, *The American Scholar*, and *Nature.*
322. **Hilary Hinton "Zig" Ziglar**: salesman, author, and motivational speaker. Zig Ziglar shared a philosophy of long-term, balanced success focusing on character, attitude, and skills. Learn more by visiting **www.ziglar.com**

323. **Steve Pavlina**: American self-help author, speaker, and creator of the very successful blog, **www.stevepavlina.com**

324. **Nike**: American corporation developing and selling athletic footwear, apparel, equipment, and accessories.

325. **Winston Churchill**: British politician best known for his leadership of the United Kingdom during the Second World War.

326. **Randy Pausch**: American professor of computer science and human-computer interaction. Before passing away of pancreatic cancer, he gave an upbeat lecture titled "The Last Lecture: Really Achieving Your Childhood Dreams". Read more at **www.thelastlecture.com**

327. **Leo Buscaglia**: aka "Dr. Love" was an author, professor, and motivational speaker. His main message was to give more love, accept more love, and open your heart to life. His books include: *Living, Loving, and Learning*, *The Way of the Bull*, and *Personhood*. Learn more at **www.buscaglia.com**

328. **W. Clement Stone**: businessman, philanthropist, and self-help author.

329. **Jack Canfield**: American motivational speaker and author. He is best known as the co-creator of the Chicken *Soup for the Soul* book series.

330. **Malcolm Forbes**: publisher of Forbes magazine.

331. **Martin Luther King, Jr**: American clergyman, activist, and prominent leader in the Civil Rights Movement.

332. **Fitzhugh Dodson**: clinical psychologist and author.

333. **Johann Wolfgang von Goethe**: German writer, artist, and politician.

334. **Phil Dunphy**: character from the television show Modern Family played by Ty Burrell.
335. **Robert M. Pirsig**: American writer, philosopher, and author. He's most well known for his book *Zen and the Art of Motorcycle Maintenance*.
336. **Benjamin Hoff**: American author who wrote *The Tao of Pooh* and *The Te of Piglet*.
337. **Dale Carnegie**: author of *How to Win Friends and Influence People* in 1936. He was a writer, lecturer, and developer of self-improvement courses. **www.dalecarnegie.com**
338. **Albert Einstein**: regarded as the father of modern physics and the most influential physicist of the 20$^{th}$ century.
339. **Unknown**
340. **Wayne Dyer**: American self-help author and motivational speaker. Learn more at **www.drwaynedyer.com**
341. **John C. Maxwell**: author, speaker, and pastor who has written more than 60 books primarily on leadership.
342. **Unknown**
343. **Lou Holtz**: retired American football coach, sportscaster, author, and motivational speaker.
344. **John Green**: New York Times best-selling author. Learn more by visiting **www.johngreenbooks.com**
345. **Marianne Williamson**: spiritual activist, author, lecturer and founder of The Peace Alliance. Learn more by visiting her website **www.marianne.com**
346. **Donald M. Kendall**: CEO of Pepsi Cola. Although this quote has also been attributed to Vince Lombardi, Vidal Sassoon, and Mark Twain.

347. **Eckhart Tolle**: best known as the author of *The Power of Now* and *A New Earth*. Learn more at **www.eckharttolletv.com**

348. **Unknown**

349. **Hilary Hinton "Zig" Ziglar**: salesman, author, and motivational speaker. Zig Ziglar shared a philosophy of long-term, balanced success focusing on character, attitude, and skills. Learn more by visiting **www.ziglar.com**

350. **Vince Lombardi**: best known as the head coach of the Green Bay Packers during the 1960s. He led them to victory in the first two Super Bowls. Learn more by visiting **www.vincelombardi.com**

351. **Andre Gide**: French author and winner of the Nobel Prize in Literature.

352. **John F. Kennedy**: 35$^{th}$ President of the United States.

353. **Malcolm Forbes**: publisher of Forbes magazine.

354. **Flavia Weedn**: author on topics of spirituality and love.

355. **Unknown**

356. **St. Francis of Assisi**: Italian Catholic friar, preacher, and one of the most venerated religious figures in history.

357. **Nelson Mandela**: served 27 years in prison before being elected president of South Africa. He also led his party in the negotiation that led to the establishment of democracy in 1994.

358. **Henry Cloud**: clinical psychologist and author of *Boundaries: When to Say Yes, How to Say No, To Take Control of Your Life*. Co-written with Dr. John Townsend. Learn more at **www.drcloud.com**

359. **Anais Nin**: French-Cuban author best known for her life and times in *The Diary of Anais Nin*, Vols. I-VII. Learn more by visiting **www.anaisnin.com**

360. **J.K. Rowling**: bestselling British novelist of the *Harry Potter* series.

361. **William Somerset Maugham**: English playwright, novelist, and short story writer.

362. **Trinidad Hunt**: author and educator helping people to reach more of their natural potential. Learn more at **www.trinidadhunt.com**

363. **Unknown**

364. **Steve Maraboli**: speaker and author on topics including inspiration, peak performance, and human potential. Learn more at **www.stevemaraboli.com**

365. **Esther Hicks**: author of *Ask and It Is Given*. Find out more by visiting **www.abraham-hicks.com**

# ABOUT THE AUTHOR

Dr. Joe Tichio has been collecting inspirational quotes for over 15 years. In 2008, he created the website Greatest-Inspirational-Quotes.com to share these amazing quotes and help inspire others to live happy, successful, and empowered lives. He is a chiropractor, rock climber, and speaker on topics including wellness, inspiration, and personal development.

If you have questions, comments, or would like to book Dr. Joe Tichio as a speaker, please contact him via email by visiting his website **www.Greatest-Inspirational-Quotes.com**.

Made in the USA
San Bernardino, CA
01 May 2015